# F

There is lore and legend that have gone by the wayside, undocumented. There are signs and wonder that only end up as folklore, because the carrier of the magic, the capsule in which it was transported, wasn't preserved. The capsule and carrier can be many things, a painter of a canvas, a sculptor of clay, a vocalist of a song, or a pen. Simply a pen. And the pen can be a voice and a verse. And the voice and verse is the most amazing while here, and most missed when gone. There are voices that are more catchy, more trendy, more stylish, and more current, but don't possess the prolonged staying power of the voice that can outlast the rises and falls of fodder. Sometimes, these voices are in the shadows and the pens are lost amongst more important documents. Sometimes, the story never translates to the big screen or past the setting of the significance. It's the significance of the voice that gives it the staying power of time. Keith Rodgers is such a voice and a pen. He is well known for founding and creating the largest and most prolific poetry collective in the world, Black On Black Rhyme. He is less well known for his pen. Yet it is his pen that found voice and called and beckoned and beaconed and bellowed and cried and commanded and beseeched and magnetized poets and griots from every nook, cranny, style, region, geography, run of the mill demographic and walk of life. With his pen, he can simultaneously modernize the ancient art of griot and canonize the current art of spoken word. With his pen, he makes light work and light feel of the real and "Too Heavy For You" topics. He can do this because Keith sounds like what your favorite grandma's couch covered in plastic feels like; what your favorite Elder leading devotion at the non-air-conditioned church you couldn't wait to leave, yet long to go back to, sounds like. Keith's pen makes you feel like what the grit cake, made from the day-old grits makes you feel: you didn't know it at the time, but you needed it. He does this with a disposition of a hustler. Nobody likes to be hustled, but everyone loves a hustler. A hustler knows this, and the best hustlers not only know this, but ensure the love stays by hustling to deliver on the promise of exceeding your expectations. Fair exchange is no robbery. This is Keith's voice and Keith's pen. Unassuming at first, but assuming you stick around for the slightest amount of time, you will soon learn why it is so significant. I first met Keith in passing, in 2001; I often called on a young lady that was his neighbor at the time. Overtime, his face became familiar to me, though I didn't know his name. I didn't know his voice or pen at the time, though I did know he was a hustler by his speech. His speech would suggest to me that I attend his open mic show. I assumed the open mic was mainly for horrible rappers wishing anyone would listen to them, because they would otherwise have no other audience. But Keith knew what I needed, just like the best hustler, or the favorite Elder or Grandma's aesthetic. The thing about griots and they are both poets and prophets. The griot is both performance and purpose. So although Keith knew what I needed, I ignored his requests for 12 months. A year later from the first time I encountered Keith, had become familiar with him enough to feel good about his energy, I saw him on an auditorium stage, doing a poem, with a voice. Immediately, I was drawn to the significance of his pen. From cadence to content, I felt at home. I felt like I could've written the poem, but I know I couldn't have written the poem because it was so damn good! I was so drawn to watching the hustler turn to homeboy turn to griot to then turn back to homeboy, I went and found him after the event. He remembered me, and told me, with the most surety and the least arrogance, that he knew he had what I needed. I would venture to that open mic and consistently plan to just listen; but the significance of this voice that beckoned poets from everywhere, would encourage me to recite my own poems. I would recite with my nose buried in a book, at first. Until Keith told me, with the most surety and least arrogance, that it was time to shed the crutch of my book and speak to much bigger stages and pen a voice of significance of my own. Keith is responsible for so many poets finding their footing, and so many griots finding out they possessed power. His pen did it first. His pen and his voice may be comparable to the artist that makes art that you can trace so that you can become your own artist one day. His pen is a magnificent familiarity and an incredible adventure that you don't know how it will end. The balance is unbelievable but this hustler, griot, Elder, and brother of mine has perfected the artform and the art of making the magical seem relatable and attainable. Now we have asked for a work like this, one that could be documented to never go by the wayside, for at least twenty years. I am too excited to finally have it here, and for it to be shared with the world. Because this pen is one of significance that can outlast any fad. This pen belongs to Keith Rodgers.

**Written by Javonte Anyabwele**

**For More Information on Keith Rodgers Scan QR Code**

**To Keith Rodgers, from the top of my heart to the bottom of my soul, Thank you for allowing me to be a consultant on this project. It is a high honor to be able to serve and be a member of Black on Black Rhyme.**

**To the supporters of this project, if you are interested in collaborating with me. I am available for:**

**Personal and Professional Development trainings**
**Keynote Speeches**
**Mastermind Groups**
**Career and Educational Consulting**
**Poetry Features**
**Poetry/ Creative Writing Workshops**

**Scan QR Code for More info**

**https://solo.to/lilarc**

Facebook: Derrick Standifer
Instagram: Lilarc_
**www.lilarc.com**

# TABLE OF CONTENTS

# Chapter I - PRIVATE SESSIONS I

**A Moment Ago**

I thought about you today
a matter of fact…a moment ago
It is an image of you in my mind
When I need a woman to hold

When I want to smile, I think about yours
Radiating like the sun from your face
When I think of you I can't stop
My mind drifts away to another place

Where you and I are walking hand in hand
Barefooted along the seashore
It's higher than heaven, sweeter than paradise &
I'm feeling emotions I've never felt before

The sun shines down upon us
I can see it's reflection in your eyes
I then kiss you softly on your lips
And raise you up toward the skies

And then I bring you back down to earth
And lower you with a kiss to the sand
You beg me to make love to you
And your wish is my command

As the sun goes down…so do I
To the sweet nectars of your passion
Your eyes sparkle in the moonlight
As you whisper "Make it everlasting"

Your breath upon my ears chills me
Like the wind stranded between the trees
You seductively blow your lips my way
And I gladly return the breeze

Two souls on the edge of ecstasy
Falling into a sea of seduction

In slow motion like hot lava
Flowing from a pleasurable eruption

Your body shakes and your body shimmers
Your moans fill the air
And I realize that I just made love to an angel
So there must be a heaven somewhere

I reach over to caress your soul
But you spread your wings and fly away
I grasp for you with desperate hands
But you say reality won't let you stay

A tear falls from your eye
And gently lands on my cheek
Lonely and crying I realize that
All the while I had been asleep

I had been captured by an enticing dream
And it refused to surrender me
Everything was so pleasant and real
But I was making love to a memory

That was on the verge of reality
Never thought anything could be so sweet
But then I became suspicious
Because of a beautiful feather on my sheet

But then I started thinking…thinking
Trying to bring some logic in on my confusion
The feather was evidence that it was you
Not some fantasy or illusion

Now every time I have sweet dreams
My love for you continues to grow
I thought about you today
A matter of fact…a moment ago

## You Make Me Feel Good

The smell of a dozen roses couldn't compare
To the scent of your presence which is quite rare
Like a thousand candies melted into you
A beautiful brew-a sexy sweet stew
An aurora about you that can't be understood
And that's why YOU MAKE ME FEEL GOOD

Chills on my conscious cooling me to a calm
The effect you have on me is like "red rum"
Dizzy with desire sometimes unaware of my actions
Driving drunk off your love steering towards satisfaction
Accidentally accelerating almost being killed
From excitement from how YOU MAKE ME FEEL

That tingling sensation underneath my skin
Has my mind wanting to go places that my body has never been
A perfect picture of paradise painted on a piano
Me stroking the keys to your needs have you moaning in soprano
Creeping and sleeping with you nothing can wake me
Because nothing relaxes me the way YOU MAKE ME

Footsteps following forever in rhythm
In a crowded room but no one can hear them
But your ears and mine tuned in together
To the sounds of heartbeats pulsing forever
I pity the people with a chance of a lifetime who wait
As I start to cry, I can't deny the love YOU MAKE

I used to long for something so strong every day of the week
The way you melt me the first time you felt me peak
Your breath upon my chest not a minute rest you continued
The heart of me the best part of me was in you
So deep you started to weep and shake too
As you started to come again like Christ, It was nice and
"Good To Feel Me Make YOU"!

**The Miracle**

My life was a catastrophe
A total shame
It could have been compared
To a hurricane

Total Destruction
Ferocious winds
Ripping my heart
Again and again

My mind was like debris
Hurled in the air
The agony I felt
Was too much to bear

Nowhere to run
Nowhere to hide
But through the terrible storm
You stood by my side

You were my umbrella
My protection from the rain
You overpowered the heartbreaks
That I had sustained

Now another day has dawned
Another day has passed
You and I lay face to face
In the splendid grass

God can work miracles
Believe me it is true
Because a miracle is what
I have found in you

**Us**

You
When I think of you
I think of how you unselfishly give
Killing me softly but yet
I Stills love to live

For the future for the present
And for the past
When I think of you
I think of glass

Through you I can see
The other side of man
That precious and fragile side
That caresses with your hands

And now it seems so clear
As if I already knew
When I think of love
I think of YOU

Me
When you're around me
Do you notice how I change
That intimacy you put into me
Makes my love come down like rain

No umbrella for this fella
Drowning in your love
And while floating in your wetness
What don't I think of

I think of closeness, friendship
And I think of security
When it comes to pleasing thee
You are the epitome

Us
Some people think it is U.S.
As in United States
Some people don't think at all
Because the feeling is too great

Some people see you and
Don't realize there is a me
Trying to separate the two
Into he and she

But you and I are tried and true
We have built each other's trust
Something rare-love and care
That perfect pair…US

**The Proposal**

I have done it a thousand times
Quietly to myself and in my mind
I've heard your answer in my dreams at night
That's why it feels so right

When I look at you and think of us
I think of love, friendship and trust
At its utmost we have achieved
A level of love that Cupid wouldn't believe

And it's not a sexual thing
Or a physical thing
It is an essential thing
A sensual thing

A feeling of companionship
That's present even when we are apart
I think it in my mind
And I can feel it in my heart

I can see it with my eyes
I can touch it with my hands
I can inhale the smell of love
That makes a man

Appreciate the smaller things in life
I have done it a thousand times
Quietly to myself and in my mind
Now I must ask you to be my wife

And together we can experience
Whatever life has in store
I'm not just asking you to be mine
But will you let me be yours

# CHAPTER II INSPIRATION

**Eyes On The Prize**

While living I have learned many things about life
The pains the gains the struggles the strife
Once a man with both of his ears missing
Sat me down and asked me to listen

He said being loved is a blessing but knowing how to love is a virtue
He said they're bad things that are good for you & some good things that will hurt you
As I nodded my head to show that I did agree
A man with no eyes said there was something he wanted me to see

He asked me to close mine so I could see through his
I saw tears fears and painful years
I heard screams from bad dreams that seemed to concern me
And then a man with no legs took me on a journey

I saw fatherless kids stealing for meals
I saw single mothers working three part-time jobs to pay the bills
I saw rich kids with everything but doing nothing wit' it
And when I was at the point of trying to get it

Along came a crazy man who said something that made sense
He said I'm not crazy just a little tense and different
He said I wear one shoe because I can't afford two
He said I talk to myself because you won't let me talk to you

He said I eat out of the trash because you're the fool who threw away a good meal
And then he asked me if I didn't have any hands how would I feel
And then he pointed to a little girl with no hands but who was dying to touch
And then a man with no tongue wrote me a note that said I talk too much

And as I sat there dumbfounded with my mouth shut
He wrote me another note that asked me to look up
And there was an image of a man with no hands or no legs
Who looked half-crazy with no ears on his head

He said son you can learn something from anyone if you just keep on trying
And you can't stop living for the fear of dying
And then he looked at me even though he didn't have any eyes
He said your life is yours to live but remember, keep your head towards the skies and KEEP YOUR EYES ON THE PRIZE

**My Intentions My Inventions**

If my words as a whole
Could half-way touch your soul
You have heard my intentions
My inventions
You see my concerns are like stains on white sheets
You try to scrub the love away with bleach
But that only makes the foundation weak
So build flowers around your fears and troubles
Water them with tears and bubbles
let the roots anchor in your heart
And let not hate tear us apart
But draw us nearer
Make things clearer
Make days brighter
Be a winner
Be a fighter
Not a quitter
And don't be bitter
Toward your enemies and foes
Be a wildflower
Instead of a rose
In an open field
Not a crowded patch
Deal with the truth
And stick to the facts
Instead of concerning yourselves with rumors and lies
Because one may seem like the other in disguise
And do remember it is not what someone lies about
But what you choose to believe
If someone tells you that the air is poisonous
It is still up to you to breathe
But if you breathe and breathe with ease
Again and again
That could have been your enemy posing as if they were chosen
To be your friend
But if you inhale and exhale and for some strange reason you die

That could have been your friend who you thought was your foe telling you a lie

So, choose your choice because your choice may be fatal
To you who are waiting to exhale hear me out while you're able
Because if my words as a whole
Half-way touch your soul
You have heard My Intentions…My Inventions

## My Poetry

If I had to write a poem about love
It would be about my mother
If I had to write a poem about excitement
It would be about my lover
Because those are the two most important
Women in my heart
But if I had to write a poem about companionship
It would be about my art
Because my poetry notices me
When no one else does
It found me when I was lost
As if it knew who I was
It tapped me on the shoulder
I turned around It shook my hand
It looked at me with sincerity
And said listen my man
If you listen to me everything
Will be just fine
Don't just write to please their bodies
You have to write to stimulate their minds
It said don't just write for the adults
You also have to write for the kids some
But knowing is plain 'ole knowledge
But how you use it is your wisdom
It said everyone sees the same thing
But how they look at it is the difference
It said for instance
If someone calls you a smart ass
Take that knowledge as a compliment
Because wisdom teaches if you weren't a smart ass
They would have to put up with some dumb shit
And with knowledge people view that life is short
But with wisdom we know that this is wrong
It's not that life is too short
It's just that death is so long
Can I move on

My poetry said an old man's lies can be the truth
And it knew that it had lost me
It said would you believe a man in a business suit
Or an old wine head with false teeth
It said son knowledge will knowingly let the Old man's false teeth mislead you
But wisdom teaches that false things can come out of someone's mouth
But yet they can still speak the truth
So you see if I had to write a poem about knowledge
I probably wouldn't write it knowingly
But if I had to write a poem about wisdom
I would write it about My Poetry

**My Sorry Ass Poem**

Brothers- who every other month they back in court
Brother who don't care take care of the kids and won't pay their child support
Sistas who have four different babies from six different guys
Sitting on the porch waiting for the mailman to arrive
The first of the month
We know what you want
Well he ain't coming just yet
Cause he ain't been
Delivering his own child support check
To the brothers who don't want to work anymore
Burglarizing people's houses and cars
And robbing people's stores
And to you sistas who 'round here got your kids calling their grand mommy, mother and
Calling you by your first name
Really need to get yourselves together
Because all y'all should feel ashamed
For being the inspiration for my sorry ass poem.

**Not Does it Matter**

Not does it matter for which I claim to be
So not different from you but not so same to me
Am I so what I seem and not so what I speaketh
Strong so are my words but yet my actions are weakest
Claim so to move mountains I know not why mountains don't budge
You're living not right judge not I not judge
To judge seems so easy but judge I not do
Scrutinized by judge me not eyes why must I be judged by you
Do not do what I do because I do not do what I say
Is not serious a slander untrue so why must you play
Misinterpreted are words between two when clearly not heard
Different story not same when passed to a third
Kept is my silence-words not harm when not spoken
Stronger be the secret when silence not broken
Diseased ears contaminated words like viruses rumors spread
Repeat not conversations genuine truth is not shed
False be the sleep true dreams may be shattered
But if the truth awakens the sleeper
NOT DOES IT MATTER

# CHAPTER III AFROCENTRIC

## Afrocentric

Afros, dreadlocks, bald heads, and braids
Afro puffs, plaits and high top fades
Afro-centric Daddy-O Afro-centric

Right on brother-what's up playa and cool cat
Fight the power and hip phrases like that
Afro-centric Daddy-O Afro-centric

Wide noses, ebony skins, and big lips
Nappy headed, bow-legged, and big hips
Afro-centric Daddy-O Afro-centric

Gospel, rap, sweet jazz, down home blues and bass
Hip-hop, reggae, and that go-go pace
Afro-centric, Daddy-O Afro-centric

Zulu, Swaheli, Ashanti
Nakema, Nefertiti, Naja, Imani
Afro-centric Daddy-O Afro-centric

Juices, berries, shells, and beads
Utilizing the earth and all of its weeds
Afro-centric Daddy-O Afro-centric

Chit'lins, bacon, grits, cornbread, and beans
Okra, yams, pig feet, oxtails, black-eye peas, and collard greens
Afro-centric Daddy-O Afro-centric

Give me five on the black hand side
Put it in the hole cause I know you got soul
Afro-centric Daddy-O Afro-centric

**I Am A Black Man**

I have walked
The long roads
I have carried
The heavy loads
That was placed upon my back
I have survived
Because I am black
I am a black man

I have survived
The slave ships
I have survived
The leather whips
That was slashed across my back
I have survived
Because I am black
I am a black man

My children have starved
Because I couldn't feed 'em
I fought many wars
But yet no freedom
Now please correct me if I'm wrong
My love for my people gave me strength
Your hate made me strong
I am a black man

I am a bastard child
Because you killed my forefathers
You raped my three mothers
And got two redbones daughter
Now I am the one
Left to do the strugglin'
And you wonder why I can't feel love again
I am a black man

I have survived
The jungles of the motherland
I have survived
The attempted genocide of my brotherman
I have survived
The police brutality
My color is my reality
I am a black man

**A Woman Black**

Kinky hair from here to there
So much hips, she needs two chairs
To sit secure, proud and pure
Mother of them all
A BLACK WOMAN y'all

Like the wind, she moves me
With love she grooves me
In sickness, she soothes me
Pushes me forward, not down
I can feel her heart pound
Through my soul making me whole
And full of love
Who am I speaking of
A BLACK WOMAN y'all

The blackest of the berries
The reddest of the cherries
And the brown cream Queen in between
An inspiration to a nation
African, Jamaican, American,
and Haitian
Skin more shades than a palm tree
And when the pressure is on me
She knows how to calm me
A BLACK WOMAN y'all

Doctors and nurses swinging purses
Lawyers and judges
Make up smudges
Single moms and housewives
Evangelist saving lives
Police keeping the peace
Janitors sweeping floors
Need I say more
They run the gamut from babysitters to architects
And all of them deserve respect

A BLACK WOMAN y'all
Professors, teachers and ballplayers
Singers, writers and rhyme sayers
Musicians and the lovers of the art
And the breaker of hearts
And the maker of homes and soul food
Classy with that sassy attitude
The setter of mahogany moods
So don't get her wrong
Made many men grown
Too much pride not to be strong
We break up to make up
But before she wakes up
She knows that I'm coming back
To my color-coded companion
MY WOMAN BLACK

She exploits a man's thoughts
Until he has to sneak to look
Stealing peeks at her mystique
As if he was a crook
She struts her stuff
Until when she walks
She slides and glides
Turning men's head
From side to side
Catching their eyes
Making them open wide
But she has nothing to hide
They have never seen a creature
With such distinct features
That when she STOps
Seems so does the Universe
But parts of her keep moving
As if it was rehearsed
But that is just her natural anatomy
And it makes me glad to be
Her opposite because we do attract
A black man and A WOMAN BLACK

**Black on Black Rhyme**

I Gets one, I Gets two because I am Ghetto
It's a poetic drive by- if you don't want to die you best get low
Even ketchup gets caught because it moves a bit slow
I try to get enriched but you still treat me as if I was a bit po'
That's why I must try to get myself a lil' bit mo'
So I won't get walked on like a foot and lose the power to heal
The soul of the ghetto
No violence, just silence in my mind
What's this? Lyrical bliss- Black on Black on Rhyme

Childhood in a wild hood but I maintained
Don't laugh, took a bath in a foot tub- NO SHAME
Been po' since I was fo' most of my friends been the same
More than once wit' no lunch- no water PLEASE RAIN
So I can catch a few drops so I can stop this thirst –
No dinner I'm getting thinner-
Situation getting worse
Daddy almost died, Momma cried,
The insurance did not pay one dime
The man tricked 'dem into being a victim of
Black On Black Rhyme
But my father was strong
He held on when he was supposed to let go
He overcame his personal pains to get us up out the ghetto
From my people I've learned when bridges burn you can
Still build mo'
You can have a good income and then some and
Still feel po'
But poverty is like a novelty that has become my friend
To be rich is great- the more you make the more you tend to spend
But when you are broke you learn to cope
With your empty pockets and wealthy mind
But as soon as you get rich you tend to forget
When you were a victim of Black on Black Rhyme

# CHAPTER IV THE DIRTY THIRTY DIVIDED BY SIX

**No Good But So Good**

If I make you feel so right
Would I be wrong
If I touch you right there-you know where
Would you moan
If I kiss you right there-you know where
Would you blush
If I lick you right there- you know where
Would your blood rush
To the spot that's burning hot
From my wet tongue
Would you lose control of your soul
And unwittingly get sprung
On the love that I be making
Have you shaking and aching
For the pleasures of a player
Have you saying a prayer
For me to safely return again
Have you acting funny around your friends
They don't understand why you do what you do
But they don't feel the thrills that I give you
And you are scared to tell them the truth
Because you say they just may want some too
Have you burning with fire and desire with no wood
They keep saying I'm no good- But I'm so good
Running my tongue up and down your spine
Exploring hot spots fire couldn't find
Getting you so high on my love you start to float
As I slowly slide my tongue down your throat
I lick my fingers to fondle your erect nipples
As beads of swollen sweat trickle
Down your chest, between your breast, down your hairline
At the same time, "You're such a rare find"
Is what I'm telling you,
Slowly smelling you
Rocking your boat and sailing you
To paradise-ecstasy-and heaven too
Our bodies are the followers,

True passion is the leader
I sprinkle sugar on your body to make you that much sweeter
Your eyes slowly close,
your legs slowly open
As I enter your loveliness,
I start stroking Deeper, Longer
Harder, Stronger with expertise
The more you get the less you need
Me directing you and guiding you
Riding you and inside of you
Is where I belong
And how could it be wrong
If I touch you right there-you know where
And made you feel sho' good
Would you think I was no good
Or so good?

**Sometimes I Wanna**

Sometimes I wanna ease
Into the whispers of a summer breeze
Cause ripples in a vast ocean
Care free with no emotion
Traveling no certain routes
When asked my whereabouts
Simply say "Yonder went he"
Blowing ever so gently

Sometimes I wanna submerge
Into every beautiful word
So you could hear
Me coming through your ear
I would softly stroke your eardrum
With the sweetest, most romantic love song
Letting you know our dreams aren't so wild
Then I would lick your lobes to make you smile

Sometimes I want to swim in your loveliness
Forever stroking never thinking of a rest
And with every stroke I would go deeper and deeper
Into your wetness until I reach your
Sweetest desires and make your waterfall
Within you and shake your sugar walls
Until all of your desires have come and gone
And then I would emerge from your pool of passion
With a moan
And simply say "Sometimes I wanna"
And one day……I'm gonna

**Rest My Head**

Baby, Baby, Baby-Can I shine
My love light on your behind
And let me call that my bright ass thought
That is, if you don't mind
Or maybe that is… if you can handle
A candle dripping hot wax on your back
While you relax and blow on my sax
Playing my favorite tune
You know when you break it down and hummmmm
Leaving me sticky like gummmmmmm
You da' bomb
You got that type of tongue
That will make a dead man come

Baby, Baby, Baby I don't mean no disrespect
But I'mma po' man
And you looking better than a welfare check
And speaking of check you can have mine
And I'm not just talking about the stub
You remind me of a speeding ticket -you fine
And I want a piece of your love
Shiiid- I'll even take a piece of your hate
Because for me that's still a come up
I know you're saying I'm so silly and crazy
But I want to be more than just one nut
Coming out of testicles flowing through vesicles
Spending the rest of my life in latex being flushed
And don't feel shame from how fast you fell for this game
Because yesterday wouldn't have been soon enough
And oh my dear I won't tell you what you want to hear
Instead I'll shoot some game to your head that you never heard
I don't just want the number to your phone
The keys to your home is what I want
So I can give you what you deserve

And if you're down with that
Should I park in the front or the back
Because I like that type of motion
And if you think I'm being too nasty
And my game is a little bit too ashy
Baby I'll bring some soap and some lotion
So write down your name and address
And what type of mattress
You sleep on because I only creep on
The best quality
I'm not trying to be smart,
but I don't do Walmart
And I damn sho' don't do Dollar Tree
Oh you don't do it on the first night
Well that's all right
Why do you think I said what I just said
Me and my girl got into a fight
And she kicked me out last night

And I just need a place to rest my head

**I Want**

I want A
I want I
Oh I want you
To tease me
So I can taunt you
With tantalizing tones
Midnight moans
Beads of sweat
Bodies shivering and wet
Sliding slowly
I want you to show me
The nasty nots
The connect the dots
Of your body parts
The canal to your heart
The blood that flow
That makes you glow
When you come and when you go
From side to side from back to front
Exploding with pleasure
That's what I want.

**Love Sucks**

Love sucks
And it sure does
Why do I say that
Because
I met this girl with some fat lips
But I'm not going to take y'all on that trip
But love sucks
Because it picks you up
And then it drops you down
That's the falling in love
Watch out for the ground
Love can be empty
And at the same time full of shit
Love can be one size fits all
And at the same time give you fits
Love can be a good card that simply misdealt
Love can be a secret that's miskept
Untold to no soul but misused and abused
You do everything to win, but yet you still lose
Because love sucks and it makes me sick
When I am in the sack with no socks
Rubbing those cold feet in the wrong sec
And you better stop
And get those ashy toes
Off my chest and off my cheeks
Baby love sucks
But love ain't me

# CHAPTER V THE FUNNIES

## Front Row Seats

I had front row seats to a concert
So I decided to take this girl from work
She gave me her address and
It was in the projects
So I went to scoop her up
After I cashed my check
We got to our seats
Her face was all aglow
She said so this is what it feels like
To sit in the front row
Where do you usually sit
Is what I asked my date
She turned around and pointed to SECTION 8.

**When You Broke**

I'm not trying to poke fun at folks
But your thinking is different when you broke
When you have yourself a pocket full of money
You are so happy until everything is funny
Hey YALL LET'S GO TO THE MALL!
You're paying off your debts and giving out loans
Although you know you don't, people think you got it going on
You know you used to go to Mickey D's to get takeout
But wait tonight you got a date and you're going to the steakhouse
HEY ROOMIES Y'ALL WANT TO RENT SOME MOVIES?!
Going to the club showing your boys love
Treating them dirty fools like superstars
"Hey boo do you think you can buy me a drink"
Get your girl cause I'm about to buy the bar
Tell your friends, after party at the Holiday Inn
The next morning you are stressed cause your finance is so much less
Than it should be and that's not good-see
All but six dollars is spent
And you forgot to pay your rent
As much as it hurts- y'all want to go to church?

**Change**

My job is killing me
But I gots to make a living
I am broke as a joke
And you can take that as a given
But beggers, hustlers, and charities
And believe me there are plenty
Constantly wanting me to donate
To them my very last penny
Although I just told them no an hour ago
They ask me again with no shame
And they are fast to say look in your ashtray
Because even spare change
And what about these changing times
Changing weather and changing seasons
Changing faces, changing places
And changing reasons
And even letters make a change
Because I changed and U changed since we've met
And oh yeah what about
The letter X
You know when you go to the store
With some stolen stuff running game
and the whole while you want a smile
When the clerk says
"Do you want a cash refund or an even ex-change"

**Rolo**

You can roll a Rolo to your pal

You can roll a rolo to your gal

It is covered with Caramel

Roll a Rolo is what I shall
Doo-oo-oo I'll roll one to you
You can roll a Rolo to your mom
You can even roll your daddy one
Roll 'em to the right and to the left
I like rolling them to myself

**Growing Up**

I was walking down the sidewalk

Along a much-traveled road

And I saw a frog nearly killed

By a car being towed

Now when you hear this next verse

You might say "what a lie"

I saw a margarine truck dodge a caterpillar

You should have seen that butterfly

A little duckling almost lost his bill

Because he almost forgot to duck

But that's all a part of changes, metamorphoses

And the process of growing up

# CHAPTER VI THE NAME GAME

**Your Name**

If I could write a poem about something warm
I would have to start with your heart
If it was my duty to create a natural beauty
What I'd simply do is draw a portrait of you
Would I be a bit naughty and draw a nude body
Or leave your treasures hidden or uncover what is forbidden
I could do a little of both to tease the eyes of folks

Who dared to take a peek of such a masterpiece

I will put you on display for only a day
After a day they won't come around cause I'll take you down
Off that wall because there is a chance you may fall

If you fall, I will break that's why I have to take
Precautions to preserve you but that's not why I deserve you
I deserve you because you want me too
And because you're sweeter than honeydew

You're beautiful like its definition
But that's not why I give you recognition
My eyes have recognized a beauty untamed

It's untitled so it's vital that I call it Your Name

**Craving Peaches**

Felt her presence only once
Eyes of gold skin of bronze
Fingers long heart so tender
Lovely legs smooth and slender
Hips are luscious with a glistening glow
My heart beats rapidly when she moves slow
And when she smiles, oh what a smile
Has my senses running wild
If she only knew how far it reaches
I find myself craving Peaches
Preserved or sweetened..um..let me see
Will she be willing to preserve that sweetness for me
I will take her whole or sliced in halves
If I licked her fingers would she laugh
Or if I licked her toes would she moan
If I did what's right would I be wrong
For giving her chills or better yet Peach fuzz
Could this be the beginning of a sweet love
Or should I stop before it gets started
Or should I go to the supermarket
To learn the lesson infatuation teaches
When I find myself craving Peaches

**Mimi, Myself and I**

Sing a song of seduction
A pocket full of kisses
For my hot chocolate desire
For my sweet black mistress

Like an innocent woman convicted
Her sex is appealing

The conviction of killing
Me softly with her feelings

Her sweetness is my freakiness
It keeps me hard as stone

My freakiness is my weakness
But I'm so strong

Between the sheets I'm a freak
But she is too

Going on all night long
'Til the morning dew

Falls upon the grass
Up from the sky

And gently lands on
Mimi, Myself, and I

**Porsche**

A Porsche-a fine-tuned machine
Long, slender, sexy, and lean
The color-a pecan tan
Only driven by a special man
A man who knows how to steer
And who can hit all five gears
While racing his hands around her curves
And who can regain control whenever she swerves
So when you ride her buckle up for safety
Like a ripe peach, looks so tasty
Burn rubber but she don't have any tires
Not for sell, don't need a buyer
Just need a man who can fit the bill
Who can hit the hills and give her thrills
Who am I-a potential Pisces
To drive this Porsche,
I have the license
It is soft to the touch and full of desire
Wet like water and hot like fire
An unhidden passion it is almost torture
It's not a car-her name is Porsche

**I've Had Michelle**

Sometimes in life
You are attracted to your opposite
Because "chance" is like a store
And I'm forever shopping it
Looking for that special something
That is quite a rarity
I earn what I get
But I do I accept charity
Now that I am a man
Matured from a boy
I've learned that I will never have happiness
Until I've had my Joy
And when I get my Joy
I will scream, shout, and yell
But I will never have Joy
Until I've had Michelle

# CHAPTER VII ISSUES

## Do You Really Care

I'm nice looking with a nice shape
But is it really my fault that I got raped
I don't twist when I walk or wink my eye
At strangers in the night while walking by
I don't flaunt my sexuality by playing love games
My innocence was taken but it is me that you blame
Through blurry eyes I see life just isn't fair
Now I am afraid to ask you…Do You Really Care?
Because if you cared you would hold me not scold me
About what I should have done and what you told me
Mother, please listen and try to understand
That I have strength, but not more than that man
I did what you said but still had no control
He raped my body and now you are raping my soul
I told you what happened, but you only stared
Now I curiously ask you…Do You Really Care?
My nightmares are true and are so vividly real
You're looking in from the outside so you can't feel
The agony and resentment inside of me now
You loved me before, but do you love me now
A mother... a daughter but are we really friends
No because I am afraid to tell you that it happened again
I want to but no…I don't dare
Because then I may find out that You Really Don't Care
Please do prove me wrong
I hope that I'm not right
Darker are my days and colder are my nights
Suicide is tempting but I'm not going to do it
All cried-out-please help me get through it
Deep down you have to care-I just know it
But the shame is it hurts me how you choose to show it
It was frightening what happened to me but the biggest scare
Is that I don't know the answer to the question of
Do You Really Care?

**Suicide**

Listen young people, suicide is not the answer
I'd rather live long and die of cancer
If you ever get depressed and all strung out
Just remember what life is all about
Self-respect, pride-just keep your stride
But the answer is not……. Suicide
You got a life to live, a lot to give
People who care friends and relatives
If you ever get discouraged and brokenhearted
Don't end your life before it gets started
We are humans and born to make mistakes
Don't give up, just give yourself a break
Suicide is a choice; some say it's sadistic
So don't you become another statistic
We are living in a world of sin
Dishonest people and dishonest friends
The pressure is on from your peers
This is no jive, you can survive so have no fears
What I'm saying is listen- listen to what I'm saying
You don't know what to do- start praying
Problems and troubles or life's side effects
But problems are just mistakes we must correct
If you commit suicide not only will it hurt you
Think of your family and friends it will hurt them too
Just because you're down now-you won't always be on the bottom
Suicide is a permanent solution to a temporary problem
It's not an accusation it's a proven fact
If you commit suicide you're not coming back

**Drunk Jiving**

You are a punk driving drunk
You can't understand
The other night you had no right
To kill that man
You didn't drive far you hit a car
The charge is manslaughter
You took the life of a wife
A son and a daughter
You have no soul you lost control
Of the steering wheel
Going around the curve you hit a girl
And she was killed
People scorned you, commercials warned you
But you wouldn't listen
You're in a cell in the county jail
Now freedom you are missing
You couldn't see -how could that be
You just weren't thinking
In the first place look at your face
You shouldn't be driving and drinking

You are filthy you know your guilty

There was an eyewitness
If they could I wish they would
Give you the maximum sentence
It's alright to drink if you think
Not to drink and drive
Like I said there are people dead
That should be alive
You did the crime now serve the time
Justice must be served
You're an alcoholic-that's what they call it
You really got some nerves
You got caught you weren't at fault

Or at least that's what you said
You started crying you know you're lying
You say you wish you were dead
A slandered name
you're still not shame
Because drinking gives you a thrill
You drank a six-pack
now you can't bring back
The people that you killed

Your trial was brief you showed no grief
What you did was a sin
Now take a look
you're off the hook
And you're drinking again
Don't take a risk
we can't leave this
Tragedy alone
Now wouldn't you hate
if the next life he takes
was your own

**Why Men Cheat**

Ahh Baby Sweets
You know why I cheat
Cause you don't play fair
Nose all in the air
Weave in your hair
Trying to get another man's attention
Don't make me mention
Them late night phone calls
Trips supposedly to the mall
Shopping with your friends
Jocking that brother with that Benz
Falling for his Mac lines
But not paying me any mind
Until you smell another woman's perfume
On my shirt in the bathroom
You say I'm ungrateful
But that's why I'm unfaithful
We met at a club, not at Church
I know why you're in pain- the truth hurts
That's why I left some pain killers and bandages on your seats
But Baby Sweets, that's why men cheat.

**Your Solution Execution**

I was an ideal citizen good job, good home
Got laid off everything went wrong
Marriage problems, couldn't solve em got divorced
Lost my house and family, the judge showed no remorse
Your Solution Execution

You killed my desire, my dream, and my hope
Sometimes a strong hearted man is too weak to cope
With the downfalls that surround y'all and him
On top of the world he's a pearl but now you can't stand him
Your Solution Execution

In the state of Florida -in a state of depression
And what is meant by the Statement "count your blessings"
He counted his money, and it came up short
Robbed a store accidentally killed the clerk- he's in court
Your Solution Execution

Now if I go to war, kill a man
I never saw and steal information
You wouldn't take my soul cause
I'd be a cold murderer for my nation
Now if I kill to live by accident or to protect myself
You want to try to control my last breath
Your Solution Execution

Now if you kill me for killing someone else
Does that not make you a killer yourself
And you do it with a smile and show no remorse
Let the death penalty take its course
With Your Solution Execution

# CHAPTER VIII THE GIFT OF LOVE

**A Rose**

Here is a gift for you
It is called love
If you accept and believe in it
You will grow
Like a rose inside my heart
I will water you with tears of happiness
And nourish you with the
Gentleness that is only expected of me
Each year, a beautiful rose
Will blossom from that bud of togetherness
And that small bud will symbolize our
Ever-growing love for each other
You see, "For God so love the world
That he gave his only begotten son and
Whosoever believeth in him shall
Not perish but have everlasting life"
I don't have a son to sacrifice
But I do have something to share with you
My love and a small token of affection...
A Rose If you would just have faith in me and trust in me
We could have everlasting love
With that in mind, we can accomplish anything we set out to do
If by chance we happen to fall short of our expectations
The experience will still be a success
Because we would still have each other and that is all we need...
EACH OTHER
You see, you are a fantasy that has emerged into reality
With that emergence came changes.
Mainly in me.
You see, you not only changed me, you changed my entire
concept about life itself.
Now I not only live for me, I live for us.
You are like a blaze burning within my heart.
Burning away the ashes of the past and in turn,
giving me light for the future.
You are truly my fire and desire.

At night I pray to the Lord to take care of you.
And each time I see your lovely face
I know that the Lord has answered my prayers
I realize how lucky I am to have a lady of your caliber in my presence and I just want to say
THANK YOU FOR THE WARMTH

**One Day More**

You are scared that I will leave you
But when will this fear stop

I wish that I could be there
To kiss away each tear drop

But I can't so I won't
Because I have a life to live too

But on the other hand
I have something that I could give to you

The reassurance of my love
And undying friendship

Even though I know you feel
That your heart has been ripped

Into so many pieces
It will be impossible to mend

But my love will be the glue for you
And just like a true friend

I will pick up the pieces
From off the floor

And for as long as you shall love me
I will love you ONE DAY MORE

**The Darkness**

Here I am, thinking about you, and all of the memories I have of
you. All of the arguments, disagreements and fights
we have had over the last five or six months.
It seems like we haven't talked for a year.
I just wrote to say hello and ask you how things are going in your
life? Well, I'm really trying to say is "I MISS YOU"! You know,
for the past four or five weeks, I didn't miss you at all.
But after I talked to you over the phone it seems like all my
feelings for you emerged from the depths of my heart. I thought
that I had finally gotten over you,
But it seems like I was wrong again, when we were talking I said to
myself, "I don't love this girl and she don't love me",
So why should I put up with this mess?
But something inside of me kept telling me to hang in there,
she will give in soon, but that never happened!
You see, I let go and you never gave in.
At that time in my life I was looking for a relationship
because I was feeling down and I was lonely and you
were the person I wanted to be around all the time.
I thought that you were the only girl in the world that had the
capability and the potential to fulfill
all my needs and wants. Girl, you loved me
and I hope you do not try to deny it. You see,
once we stopped communicating, I realized that
you cared for me, but you showed it in a different manner that I
had anticipated. Your absence brought pain and agony into my life,
The pain and agony brought me maturity and
that is what brought me out of THE DARKNESS!

**The One Who Is Falling**

I guess that this is really goodbye for you and I.
Somehow it still doesn't seem true, I guess that you leaving is something that I just got to accept. I had to accept the fact that the experience we shared together was not a dream, if it was –I wish that I had never awakened from it because reality seems like a never ending nightmare. I wish I could just hold you in my arms and rock you to sleep and dream forever. The only time that we would awaken is so that I can tell you that I love you even more.
I guess that you know that it could never be like that. So, you ask me why not? Well, you see, it is called DEPARTURE! You see, when I arrived in your life someone very close to your heart had just departed, when he came back into your life… someone very close to my heart departed. Now that happened twice upon a time and each departure was a burden to me mentally and physically! You see a man tries to hide his pain and sorrow, that is what some people call masculinity. I loved you and I can say with true honesty-I never stopped loving you. It's quite difficult to stop loving a woman of your caliber.
You are a lady with integrity and true character.
I find it virtually impossible to not love someone so lovely and sweet.
You are truly one in a million but like always-good things must come to an end. I guess you've come to realize, like myself, that life is a game of holding on and letting go, and when you were faced with that dilemma …I AM THE ONE WHO IS FALLING!

**The Inside**

I am making this up as I go
So join the ride
While I give you a peep
Of the inside
The inside is the opposite of out
Let me explain what I am talking about
Explaining,
not complaining,
attitudes collide
It's pouring down raining, let's go inside
I never showed my outward feelings

And you thought that love died
But you were truly mistaken
You should have taken a peep inside
Of my heart before you started to criticize
Then and only then you would have realized
The reason that you couldn't remember
One time that I have actually cried
No tears to wipe away from my eyes
Because they are all in the inside

# A WORD FROM THE AUTHOR

This book of poems was originally released in 1997. Before there was a poetry show called Black On Black Rhyme. Before there was a movement called Black On Black Rhyme. There was this collection of poems entitled Black On Black Rhyme! I hope you enjoyed reading this as much as I enjoyed writing this. This book will be followed by "Giant Midgets" which was released in 1998.

I also have 2 poetry cd's available
1. National Po' Day
2. Ashley's Father

I am available for Hosting, Promoting, Consulting, Speaking, Comedy, Acting, Event Planning and Facilitating Creative Writing Workshops!

I sincerely hope that you find an open mic venue near you and support it by attending and sharing their information amongst your family and friends. Better yet, I hope you find the courage to get on that mic and open up! Writing is very therapeutic! There are pages in this book that were intentionally left blank. They are for you to write a poem, thoughts, critiques or your favorite lines. Let them not be blank forever.

Made in the USA
Columbia, SC
19 May 2023

16889373R00046